31 Days to Twitter Mastery

Creating a Mostly Automated,

Highly Effective Twitter Presence

for Your Business

31 Days to Twitter Mastery

Creating a Mostly Automated,
Highly Effective Twitter Presence
for Your Business

Darlene Hull

Copyright © 2012 by Darlene Hull

No part of this publication may be reproduced, stored in a retrieval system, or transmitted, in any form, or by any means, electronic, mechanical, photocopying, recording, or otherwise, without the prior consent of the publisher.

PLEASE READ CAREFULLY

Any content, information and any materials provided in this message is on an "as is" basis. The author makes no warranty, expressed or implied, as to its accuracy, completeness or timeliness, or as to the results to be obtained by recipients, and shall not in any way be liable to any recipient for any inaccuracies, errors or omissions herein.

The author is not responsible for either the content, or output, of external websites.

This book is not sponsored or in any way endorsed by Twitter®

Cover Design: Tina Hull, Pulse Studio Graphics, www.pulsestudio.ca

Author Photo: Alexandra Bergmann, Alexandra Danae Photography

Dedication:

This book is dedicated to Candy Gage whose enthusiasm and support have given me courage to move forward and face my business challenges head on.

I love having my very own cheerleader!

Acknowledgements:

I am unspeakably grateful for my husband Tom for putting up with my crazy projects, my less than stellar domestic skills, and my frenetic personality. You are my rock and my wings and I am so blessed to have you by my side.

I am also delighted to have the honour of being skillfully raised by my two teenagers, Simon and Tina, who have taught me the joy of learning and discovery, and who put up with my ability to have three conversations in the span of a single sentence. Thanks for picking up the slack in housework, cooking, computer tech, and graphics.

You guys are a gift.

Do you have a Twitter account but aren't sure what to do with it?

Are you running your Twitter account but not seeing any success?

Are you someone who's heard about Twitter but hasn't a clue as to what it's all about?

Are you just too overwhelmed with everything else to figure this out too?

"31 Days to Twitter Mastery" is your life boat.

Every day you have one lesson that takes you step by step through the process of setting up an almost entirely automated but highly effective Twitter account that will be fun to run and vastly improve your reach and credibility in your industry.

So, take a deep breath, turn off your phone, close the office door, put on some great music, and sit down at your computer with this book. 31 days from now you'll be a Twitter pro, and wonder how you ever managed without it!

Table Of Contents

Introduction..11

Day 1 - Setting Up Your Tweet List - Quotes...........................15

Day 2 - Setting Up Your Tweet List: Cute and Funny............17

Day 3 - Setting Up Your Tweet List - Tips...............................19

Day 4 - Setting Up Your Tweet List - Other Articles..............23

Day 5 - Setting Up Your Tweet List - Questions.....................27

Day 6 - Setting Up Your Twitter Profile Page.........................33

Day 7 - Automating with Timely.is...37

Day 8 - Connecting Your Blog To Your Twitter Stream........39

Day 9 - Adding Other Blogs To Your Twitter Stream............41

Day 10 - Writing Ads For Your Twitter Stream......................43

Day 11 - Auto-posting Your Ads to Twitter.............................45

Day 12 - Setting Up Google Reader..47

Day 13 - Setting Up Follow Automation..................................49

Day 14 - Finding Followers Through Twitter Search.............51

Day 15 - Connecting With New Followers...............................53

Day 16 - Finding Followers Through Twellow........................55

Day 17 - Daily Engagement Activities......................................57

Day 18 - Setting Up Tweetdeck..59

Day 19 - Creating Twitter Lists..61

Day 20 - Scheduling Google Reader Articles With Hootsuite...............63

Day 21 - Catch Up and Connect..67

Day 22 - Cleaning Out Your Follower List..............................69

Day 23 - Tweet Your Old Posts..71

Day 24 - Create a Twitter Poll..73
Day 25 - Share a Picture...75
Day 26 - Join Klout...77
Day 27 - Adjusting Tweets Through Timely.is......................................79
Day 28 - Create an Online Newspaper...81
Day 29 - Set Up a Listening a Listening Station....................................85
Day 30 - Becoming Influential..87
Day 31 - What Else Can I Do With Twitter?...91
It's a Wrap!..93
How Might We Help You?...95

Introduction

So, you want to get started with (or improve your presence on) Twitter. Congratulations!

Twitter can be a lot of fun, and a great way to get your message out there! However, in order to be effective you have to be clear on what your specific goals are for being on Twitter, and you have to be willing to put some effort into it daily. There is no such thing as automated riches. Trust me. There are, however, ways to make things much easier.

Parts of Twitter can be automated in order to create the kind of engagement you need to reach your Twitter goals without it sucking up every available minute in your day. I've set this course up to walk you through the best way I've found of doing this for free. All you have to do is set aside about an hour a day to begin with, and work through one lesson at a time. When you're done you'll have a powerful Twitter marketing system that's about 85% automated, and you'll know how to use the remaining 15% most effectively.

If, at any time, you need help working through this, we are available at: 1-403-374-0167(MT) or via email at: info@hotspotpromotion.com.

Before we jump into the nitty-gritty there are two things to keep in mind:

1. You will need to set aside an hour a day for the next 31 days to get this done.

2. While you're free to jump around and just look at the chapters that interest you, I would suggest that wherever you are with your Twitter account, starting at the beginning of this and moving systematically forward will give you MUCH better results than treating this course as a smorgasbord.

Also, before you begin, it's important that you have a context for doing this. Marketing tactics should never be set up in a vacuum. They need be part of an overall strategy that makes sense for your business. The various pieces should all connect together. Before you get started, make sure you understand clearly the picture that Twitter is going to play in your marketing strategy.

For example:

1. What are you hoping to achieve with a Twitter account?
2. Who is your target market? If you don't know, or don't even know what I'm talking about, download our free report called "Who Are You Talking To?" right here: HotSpotPromotion.com/Target
3. Is your target market already on Twitter? If not, you're wasting your time. If so, what kinds of things are they interested in doing on Twitter? That's what you need to learn to tap into.
4. How will you define "success" on Twitter? What do you want Twitter to do - announce your promotions? Increase clicks to your website? Handle customer service? Build Buzz? It's important to go into Twitter with a clear understanding of what "success" means.
5. How will you define "failure" on Twitter, and what will you do if/when that happens?
6. How much time are you able/willing to invest into making Twitter a success? 30 minutes a day is pretty much your minimum, so keep that in mind.

Having answers to these questions will help you better prepare the information you're going to need to make Twitter as successful as possible. This course is going to help you automate all the parts of Twitter marketing that can be automated, but you're still going to have to be willing to come alongside and actually engage with your followers for Twitter to create the kind of success you're probably looking for. fully-automated Twitter account is absolutely possible. An *effective*, fully-automated Twitter account is unlikely. Social media is all about "social" so you need to make sure that you have time to engage and interact with your Twitter followers. Following the steps of this course will make sure that you have the most amount of time possible to do this well, and I'll give you some great ideas for making that happen.

So, are you ready? Let's begin!

Day 1

Setting Up Your Tweet List - Quotes

Welcome to Day 1 of "*31 Days to Twitter Mastery*"! Thanks for trusting me with your time - I promise not to waste it!

So, having said that, let's jump right in, shall we?

I don't know if you have a Twitter account or not, but if you don't you won't need one yet. We'll be setting that up on day 6. First we're going to make sure you actually have something to post that engages your (potential) followers.

Twitter is most effective if you post things that interest others while making yourself look like a warm and friendly expert. Posting a whole string of ads is going to help no one, and will likely get you banned. The nature of Twitter's fast-moving stream requires that you post frequently enough that people keep seeing your name, and seeing it attached to something interesting, informative, entertaining, and somewhat personal, that lets your personality and expertise shine through.

Here's how we're going to making that happen:

- ➢ Open up a blank Word document on your computer.
- ➢ Set up a numbered list.
- ➢ Go to Google and do a search for great quotes in your field; for example: "Great golf quotes", "Great small business quotes", "Great health and fitness quotes", "Great money quotes", "Great parenting quotes" Whatever you search for should appeal to your ideal target market.

- ➢ Copy and paste an quotes that are 120 characters or less onto your document so it looks like this:

    1. You can talk to a fade but a hook won't listen. - Lee Trevino

    2. "I have a tip that can take five strokes off anyone's golf game: It's called an eraser." - Arnold Palmer

    3. The ball retriever is not long enough to get my putter out of the tree. - Brian Weis

    4. etc,

- ➢ Keep going until you have 100 quotes on your list. Do it fast and focused. Make sure the quotes aren't rude or offensive. Humour is great if you can find funny ones

- ➢ If you can't find enough quotes in your chosen field, pick a second topic that relates well to it. For example, if you run out of "money" quotes, look for "frugal" or "finance" or "make money" or something like that..

- ➢ Save your list as "TimelyTweets". I'll tell you why later.

OK, go do it! I'll see you back here tomorrow with another lesson!

Day 2

Setting Up Your Tweet List: Cute and Funny

So, did you get your 100 quotes yesterday? It's tedious now, but once you have these 31 days completed, Twitter will be a breeze, and will likely become your favourite marketing medium!

Today's assignment:

- Create an account at bit.ly, go to the drop-down menu right at the very top next to your username, and click "tools" and drag the bookmarklet to your menu bar. Instructions are on the page.

- Open yesterday's "TimelyTweets" document

- Put a space between each quote so it looks like this:
  1. You can talk to a fade but a hook won't listen. -Lee Trevino
  2.
  3. "I have a tip that can take five strokes off anyone's golf game: It's called an eraser." - Arnold Palmer
  4.
  5. The ball retriever is not long enough to get my putter out of the tree. - Brian Weis
  6.
  7. etc,

- Go to Google and do a search for funny videos, funny pictures, articles. Anything to make people laugh. Make sure they're not rude, sexual, racist, or in any other way offensive. Look for pure clean fun. Pictures and videos that are adorably cute can also work!

➢ When you've found something great to share click your bit.ly bookmarklet, and copy the title and link from the little box it creates on the right, and paste onto your list. Reformat the title if necessary, and add a short note from yourself explaining what it is or your reaction to it.

1. You can talk to a fade but a hook won't listen. - Lee Trevino

2. **Dog vs. Leaves Video http://bit.ly/ynYstW Hilarious**

3. "I have a tip that can take five strokes off anyone's golf game: It's called an eraser." - Arnold Palmer

4. **Some people need a life: http://youtube/60og9gwKh1o Very funny!**

5. The ball retriever is not long enough to get my putter out of the tree. ~ Brian Weis

6. **Adorable Baby Sloth! http://youtu.be/Pqio2G_Ra6g**

7. etc,

Keep going until you have 100 funny/cute things on your list. Things that are clever are also useful - like a Ted talk, or something from RSA Animates. Ideally these should resonate with you - don't just post links for the sake of posting links. You're trying to draw people in, so make sure that what you're sharing has something to do with who you are, and what tickles your fancy.

You can ask people what their favourite video is, or funny story or cute picture, etc. and add their favourites to your list as well.

Save your list and we'll come back to it with new stuff, tomorrow.

Day 3

Setting Up Your Tweet List - Tips

Well, your list is starting to flesh out a little now, isn't it? We're going to keep working at it today.

Today's assignment:

➢ Open yesterday's "TimelyTweets" document.

➢ Put a space after each question and add a hashtag using your main keyword(s), for example: "#GolfTip:", "#MoneyTip:", "#FitnessTip:" etc. Create something with your keyword and put "#" in front of it, so you can easily be found in searches. There should be no spaces.

➢ Your list should now look like this:

1. You can talk to a fade but a hook won't listen. - Lee Trevino

2. Dog vs. Leaves Video http://bit.ly/ynYstW Hilarious

3. **#Golf Tip:**

4. "I have a tip that can take five strokes off anyone's golf game: It's called an eraser." - Arnold Palmer

5. Some people need a life: http://youtu.be/60og9gwKh1o Very funny!

6. **#Golf Tip:**

7. The ball retriever is not long enough to get my putter out of the tree. - Brian Weis

8. Adorable Baby Sloth! http://youtu.be/Pqio2G_Ra6g

9. **#Golf Tip:**

➤ Go to Google and do a search for quick tips in your area of focus "quick tips to save money", "quick fitness tips", "quick nutrition tips", "quick business tips", "quick marketing tips", etc.

➤ Copy and paste any tips that are 120 characters or less next to those hashtags on your document so it looks like this:

1. You can talk to a fade but a hook won't listen. - Lee Trevino

2. Dog vs. Leaves Video http://bit.ly/ynYstW Hilarious

3. **#GolfTip: You'll actually hit better golf shots in bare feet than with your shoes and socks on.**

4. "I have a tip that can take five strokes off anyone's golf game: It's called an eraser." - Arnold Palmer

5. Some people need a life: http://youtu.be/60og9gwKh1o Very funny!

6. **#GolfTip: Straight shot? Make certain the buttons on your shirt are square to the ball at setup, & again at & through impact.**

7. The ball retriever is not long enough to get my putter out of the tree. - Brian Weis

8. Adorable Baby Sloth! http://youtu.be/Pqio2G_Ra6g

9. **#Golf Tip: To maximize coil, don't lift your left foot on the backswing. (Very important, the lower body has to stay solid during the backswing.)**

Again, you want to work quickly with focus, and strive to get 100 tips in place.

Once you're done save it, and put it away until tomorrow! We'll add more fun Tweets to it then!

Day 4

Setting Up Your Tweet List - Other Articles

OK, let's dive right into our TimelyTweets list again, and add some new stuff!

Today's assignment:

- ➤ Open yesterday's "TimelyTweets" document.

- ➤ Put a space after each hash-tagged tip so it looks like this:

    1. You can talk to a fade but a hook won't listen. - Lee Trevino

    2. Dog vs. Leaves Video http://bit.ly/ynYstW Hilarious

    3. #GolfTip: You'll actually hit better golf shots in bare feet than with your shoes and socks on.

    4.

    5. "I have a tip that can take five strokes off anyone's golf game: It's called an eraser." - Arnold Palmer

    6. Some people need a life: http://youtu.be/60og9gwKh1o Very funny!

    7. #GolfTip: When you want to hit the ball straight, make certain that the buttons on your shirt are square to the ball at setup, and again at and through impact.

    8.

9. The ball retriever is not long enough to get my putter out of the tree. - Brian Weis

10. Adorable Baby Sloth!
    http://youtu.be/Pqio2G_Ra6g

11. #Golf Tip: To maximize coil, don't lift your left foot on the backswing. (Very important, the lower body has to stay solid during the backswing.)

12.

13. etc.,

➢ Go to Google and do a search for great articles, blogs, videos and the like that have to do with other areas of interest for you. You want to connect with people on a number of different levels. If your market is golfers but you're also a cat fanatic, you'll attract other golfers that are cat fanatics, and have two areas of connection instead of just one. This is the kind of post that makes you a person rather than just a marketer. So, research articles in 3-5 other areas that fascinate you, and find 100 that show the other sides of your personality.

➢ When you've found something great to share click your bit.ly bookmarklet, and copy the title and link from the little box at the top. You might have to reformat this so it looks nice. Usually it's perfect.

➢ You also want to see if the person who wrote it has a Twitter account. If so, you want to include their Twitter handle.

➢ Copy and paste these links after the tips you have on your document, along with any Twitter handles, so it looks like this:

1. You can talk to a fade but a hook won't listen. - Lee Trevino

2. Dog vs. Leaves Video http://bit.ly/ynYstW Hilarious

3. #GolfTip: You'll actually hit better golf shots in bare feet than with your shoes and socks on.

4. Cat Personality Quiz http://bit.ly/w1rVHw @CATeditor

5. "I have a tip that can take five strokes off anyone's golf game: It's called an eraser." - Arnold Palmer

6. Some people need a life: http://youtu.be/60og9gwKh1o Very funny!

7. #GolfTip: When you want to hit the ball straight, make certain that the buttons on your shirt are square to the ball at setup, and again at and through impact.

8. Sport Fishing BC - Fish Tales. Fishing stories from anglers in British Columbia http://bit.ly/yCYZRl @FishNut

9. The ball retriever is not long enough to get my putter out of the tree. - Brian Weis

10. Adorable Baby Sloth! http://youtu.be/Pqio2G_Ra6g

11. #Golf Tip: To maximize coil, don't lift your left foot on the backswing. (Very important, the lower body has to stay solid during the backswing.)

12. The Structures of Antique Lace: A Personal Collection. Bobbin Lace, Needlepoint Lace, and Other Handmade Laces http://bit.ly/yIC1Vz

Keep going until you have 100 articles on your list. Again, if you're having trouble, work at this over time, but make sure you schedule time for it daily until you have all the articles you need on this list.

Save your list and we'll come back to it with new stuff again tomorrow!

Day 5:

Setting Up Your Tweet List - Questions

We're almost done with this list. Let's dive right in and finish it up today!

Today's assignment:

➢ Open yesterday's "TimelyTweets" document (this is the last assignment with this list, I promise!)

➢ Put a space after each article so it looks like this:

1. You can talk to a fade but a hook won't listen. - Lee Trevino

2. Dog vs. Leaves Video http://bit.ly/ynYstW Hilarious

3. #GolfTip: You'll actually hit better golf shots in bare feet than with your shoes and socks on.

4. Cat Personality Quiz http://bit.ly/w1rVHw @CATeditor

5.

6. "I have a tip that can take five strokes off anyone's golf game: It's called an eraser." - Arnold Palmer

7. Some people need a life: http://youtu.be/60og9gwKh1o Very funny!

8. #GolfTip: When you want to hit the ball straight, make certain that the buttons on your shirt are square to the ball at setup, and again at and through impact.

9. Sport Fishing BC - Fish Tales. Fishing stories from anglers in British Columbia http://bit.ly/yCYZRl @FishNut

10. The ball retriever is not long enough to get my putter out of the tree. - Brian Weis

11. Adorable Baby Sloth! http://youtu.be/Pqio2G_Ra6g

12. #Golf Tip: To maximize coil, don't lift your left foot on the backswing. (Very important, the lower body has to stay solid during the backswing.)

13. The Structures of Antique Lace: A Personal Collection. Bobbin Lace, Needlepoint Lace, and Other Handmade Laces http://bit.ly/yIC1Vz

14. etc.

➢ Now you're going to fill in those blanks with two different kinds of questions. First, you're going to look for "ice-breaker" type questions. These should be simple and fun, and are there to help you engage with your followers in a way that brings out their personality, and starts short little conversations that hopefully create a laugh or two. You find these by doing a search for "Ice-breaker questions". These are the kinds of questions you should be looking for:

1. If you could be one for just 24 hours, what cereal box cartoon character would you be? Why?

2. What was the best thing that happened to you this weekend?

3. What is your favorite animal? List three adjectives to explain your choice.

➢ You want to find 50 of these, and put them in every SECOND space on your list, like this:

1. You can talk to a fade but a hook won't listen. - Lee Trevino

2. Dog vs. Leaves Video http://bit.ly/ynYstW Hilarious

3. #GolfTip: You'll actually hit better golf shots in bare feet than with your shoes and socks on.

4. Cat Personality Quiz http://bit.ly/w1rVHw @CATeditor

5. **If you could be one for just 24 hours, what cereal box cartoon character would you be? Why?**

6. "I have a tip that can take five strokes off anyone's golf game: It's called an eraser." - Arnold Palmer

7. Some people need a life: http://youtu.be/6Oog9gwKh1o Very funny!

8. #GolfTip: When you want to hit the ball straight, make certain that the buttons on your shirt are square to the ball at setup, and again at and through impact.

9. Sport Fishing BC - Fish Tales. Fishing stories from anglers in British Columbia http://bit.ly/yCYZRl @FishNut

10.

11. The ball retriever is not long enough to get my putter out of the tree. - Brian Weis

12. Adorable Baby Sloth! http://youtu.be/Pqio2G_Ra6g

13. #Golf Tip: To maximize coil, don't lift your left foot on the backswing. (Very important, the lower body has to stay solid during the backswing.)

14. The Structures of Antique Lace: A Personal Collection. Bobbin Lace, Needlepoint Lace, and Other Handmade Laces http://bit.ly/yIC1Vz

15. **What was the best thing that happened to you this week?**

➢ Your next search will be for 50 questions about your main topic of interest - golf, making money, fitness, or whatever your main theme is for your Twitter stream. These you insert into the blanks that are left, like this:

1. You can talk to a fade but a hook won't listen.~ Lee Trevino

2. Dog vs. Leaves Video http://bit.ly/ynYstW Hilarious

3. #GolfTip: You'll actually hit better golf shots in bare feet than with your shoes and socks on.

4. Cat Personality Quiz http://bit.ly/w1rVHw @CATeditor

5. If you could be one for just 24 hours, what cereal box cartoon character would you be? Why?

6. "I have a tip that can take five strokes off anyone's golf game: It's called an eraser." - Arnold Palmer

7. Some people need a life: http://youtu.be/60og9gwKh1o Very funny!

8. #GolfTip: When you want to hit the ball straight, make certain that the buttons on your shirt are square to the ball at setup, and again at and through impact.

9. Sport Fishing BC - Fish Tales. Fishing stories from anglers in British Columbia http://bit.ly/yCYZRl @FishNut

10. **What's your favourite brand of club and why?**

11. The ball retriever is not long enough to get my putter out of the tree. ~ Brian Weis

12. Adorable Baby Sloth! http://youtu.be/Pqio2G_Ra6g

13. #Golf Tip: To maximize coil, don't lift your left foot on the backswing. (Very important, the lower body has to stay solid during the backswing.)

14. The Structures of Antique Lace: A Personal Collection. Bobbin Lace, Needlepoint Lace, and Other Handmade Laces http://bit.ly/yIC1Vz

15. What was the best thing that happened to you this weekend?

16. etc.

And that's it for this list. Woohoo! You'll love me for it later, though! Tomorrow I'm going to help you set up a great Twitter page. Even if you have a page already there are probably a few things you can learn, so make sure you show up ready to work.

Oh, and you'll need a great head shot of yourself. Between now and tomorrow get a friend with a camera to take a bunch of them so you have a few good ones to choose from.

Day 6:

Setting Up Your Twitter Profile Page

Today we get to set up your Twitter page. If you've already got one just use this as a checklist to make sure you've done the best possible job of setting this up. If your page is unattractive and off-putting, or not filled out properly, it won't do the job it's intended to do.

Let's get started:

- Go to www.twitter.com and fill out the fields on the right side of the screen.

- Input your first and last name (not initials or nickname).

- Input your email address (you can log into twitter using either your email address or username).

- Input a password (6 or more characters).

- Click on 'Sign up for Twitter'.

- On the next page you'll have a chance to verify/correct your information. Change what you need to, and when you're happy with it, click "Create My Account".

    Note:

    Twitter creates a default username for you but you can overwrite it and put in the one you want to better describe your business or use a variation of your name (BobSmith, BSmith). Feel free to use great keywords (BobTheGolfer), using upper and lower case, but avoid underscores and numbers.

Keep it short, sweet, and memorable, but also keep it meaningful. Don't use something obscure like "PennyArcade" if you want to build a business with it. You have a maximum of 15 characters, but the longer your username, the more difficult it will be to get retweets as it takes up part of the total of characters - know what I mean? Short is best. Twitter will tell you if your username is taken or not.

- Read the terms of service and click "Create my account" and watch for the email to confirm your account.

- Once you've confirmed your account, login and in the upper right corner of the screen you'll see an arrow next to your username. Click on that, and then click on "Settings".

- From Settings you'll see tabs to edit. Make decisions regarding your privacy that are comfortable for you, but do make sure, if you're using this for business, that your posts are visible publicly, otherwise you're wasting your time.

- Click "profile" and chose a picture for your profile. It should be of your face, and it should be cheerful and professional. Don't have a photo there that looks like a mug shot, or like you lost your last friend, or you have no sense of style. It needs to be warm and welcoming. This is where you make your first impression. Do it well..

- Check your first and last name.

- Type your city and province.

- Include a link to your website or blog (include http://). Don't use a shortlink like http://bit.ly/njErZK instead of http://www.HotSpotPromotion.com. If you're promoting an affiliate site with a long ugly link purchase an appropriate domain name and forward it to your affiliate page so you have a tidy link.

- Include a short bio of yourself (160 characters max.) Use keyword strategy including location, name, and company. Do a search on Google for "best Twitter bios" and allow them to inspire you. Don't panic about this - remember you can always come back and change it - just don't "throw something together". Take time to craft this well.

- Avoid the use of emoticons, Twitterspeak ("UR" instead of "you are"), slang, and jargon. If possible include something personal or slightly humorous.

- Create a great background. You have three options here:

    1. You can use a single picture and tile it or span it if it's big enough as your background.

    2. You can use one of the free or paid background services. Search for "Twitter Backgrounds" to get some resources for this.

    3. You can hire it out - we'd be happy to create one for you!

And there you have it - a stunning Twitter page, sure to attract the right people to you.

Tomorrow we start posting, but feel free to put up a "hello" post if this is a brand new page!

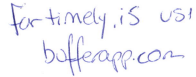

Day 7:

Automating with Timely.is

Now to get started on some of that automation I promised you! We will be setting up a few different automation tools. I know there are tools that "do it all" but there are two reasons why I'm not using them:

1. They cost money, and for small businesses, if you don't have to give out money, so much the better.

2. They require a very well organized list of posts so that you don't overwhelm or underwhelm with ads. Also, they can only be posted at certain intervals, and you can't change them on the spur of the moment if you have them all programmed in. Using the method I show costs nothing, allows you huge flexibility and needs a lot less maintenance.

Let's get started!

➢ Go to Timely.is and create an account for your new Twitter page.

➢ Once you've confirmed your account, log in and click "Settings" on the left under your Twitter name.

➢ Click whether you want to post through the weekend or not (I suggest yes to weekends), how many posts a day (I suggest 5) and then set your time zone.

➢ Copy and paste as many of your posts from your new Twitter list as you can stand. I would suggest starting with 50. So, highlight 50 posts on your list, remove the numbering on those, and start copying them into Timely.is. Timely.is will now post them throughout the day for as many days as you have filled up. It will send you an email when you run short. By removing the numbering on the posts you're entering you always know where to start the next time. Once all the numbering is gone you highlight the list, add the numbering back in, and start entering them again from the top.

➢ Looking at your schedule, decide how often you want to do this (I have chosen monthly for myself) and schedule in time to enter in enough posts to cover this time period (31x5=155 posts). Block off time on a regular basis to get this done. If you're really on top of things, you could schedule half a day and get all 500 Tweets in there if you have your list completely filled out.

As I mentioned before, if you've done your list well, when it's finished you simply start again from the beginning. Traffic moves so quickly on Twitter that it would be highly unlikely that anyone remembered what you already posted. As you get answers to some of your questions, or come across great things as you work your business, you can simply add them to this list so that it's always growing.

That's it for today. Tomorrow we begin the work to add another layer of automation to your Twitter account that's completely "hands off". Pretty nice.

Day 8:

Connecting Your Blog To Your Twitter Stream

Today we're going to step up the automation just another small notch. Today's task is only helpful if you already have a blog. If you don't already have a blog, you might want to think about starting one up. This is not something I can go into here, so let me recommend this free resource as a starting place: "**Where Are You? Creating Your Online Presence**" at HotSpotPromotion.com/website

If you do have a blog, follow these instructions:

➢ Go to www.Twitterfeed.com and open an account and confirm your email.

➢ Log in to your Twitterfeed account:

➢ Click "Create New Feed" on the top right.

➢ Type in the name of your blog.

➢ Paste your feed URL in the box, and click "Test rss feed" to make sure it's working. If you don't know where to find your feed, search "How to find an rss feed" in Google and follow the instructions.

➢ Click "Advanced Settings".

➢ Where it says "Shorten Link" choose "bit.ly" and then click bit.ly settings. Find the information you need by following these steps:

➢ Open a new tab in your browser.

1. Go to bit.ly and log in.

2. Click the drop-down arrow at the top right of your page next to your profile picture.

3. Click "Settings" and scroll down to "API Key" and copy that number.

4. Go back to Twitterfeed and paste it in - you only have to do this once!

➢ Click "Continue to step 2" at the bottom of the page.

➢ Choose Twitter, and connect the two by clicking "Authenticate Twitter". If you have any of the other accounts listed, by all means, connect your blog to those as well.

➢ Click "Create Service".

Now your blog will regularly post to all the places you just set up, without you doing a thing.

And that's it for today! Well done!

Day 9:

Adding Other Blogs To Your Twitter Stream

Today we're going to continue with Twitterfeed, but add a new twist. Instead of just promoting your own blog, you're going to find the 5 best blogs for your target market (besides your own!) So, if you're into golfing, you might be looking at a clothing store blog, an equipment blog, a skills blog, etc.

If you're into building a business, look for other blogs that help your target market in a complimentary way to what you do. For example, look for sites that do marketing, offer e-books for your market, maybe some great social media blogs to help your downline create good presence.

If you're into making money, look at ways to save, spend better, manage your investments, etc. See what I mean? What other sites can you find that your target market visits that will make you look great?

They don't always have to be in your direct area. If you run a nanny service your target market is parents, so you can simply share some of the top parenting blogs, or blogs with great recipes, for example

Here's how to do that:

> ➢ Do a search on Google for the top five blogs in your area of business: Top Social Media Blogs, Top Home Business Blogs, Top Parenting Blogs, Top Coaching Blogs. Whatever area your ideal client is most interested in that compliments your industry, find the top five blogs.

> ➢ As you open each blog, look for the RSS feed. If you don't know how to find this, search for "where do I find a blog's RSS feed?" When you find the feed, copy it.

➢ Go to your Twitterfeed account:

1. Click "Create New Feed".

2. Type in the name of the blog.

3. Paste the feed URL in the box, and click "Test rss feed" to make sure it's working.

4. Click "Advanced Settings".

5. Where it says "Shorten Link" choose "bit.ly" (this was set up yesterday).

6. Where it says "Post Suffix" put in "RT @TwitterHandle" for the person who owns the blog ("RT @Praisewalker", "RT @HotSpotPromo" etc).

7. Click "Continue to step 2".

8. Choose Twitter and connect the two by clicking "Authenticate Twitter".

9. Click "Create Service".

I wouldn't set these up for anything other than Twitter at this point. Twitter can handle a great deal of information. Most of the other social media accounts can't.

➢ Continue these steps for all five blogs. They will now post regularly to your Twitterfeed with a link back to the author's Twitter, exposing you to lots of people who follow these blogs. This also helps to create interesting updates on your own stream.

Keep an eye on these, however. Sometimes you'll notice a string of ads coming from a blog, or information that's not too useful. Just delete those Tweets. Also, you might find they post too often and then you just need to log back into Twitterfeed, select the blog that's causing the problem, go into "Advanced Settings" and set the blogging rhythm to once a day or whatever works best for you with that particular blog.

You're done! Have a good stretch and a tall glass of water!

Day 10:

Writing Ads For Your Twitter Stream

OK, now let's get down to brass tacks with regards to actually advertising your business.

While it's important to not be plugging your business with every Tweet, you do have to let people know what it is you have to offer. One way (the best way, if done correctly) is through your blog. The second way is through a variety of great ads that show up throughout your stream of other very interesting, thought-provoking items.

We're going to get started on this today by creating a super-attractive "Unique Selling Proposition" for your business. This is the most important part of the job, because it will help you understand just what it is you do, and why you're the one to do it. Download a free worksheet on how to create a USP called "**What's So Special About You?**" at www.HotSpotPromotion.com/usp.

When you are working through your USP see how many ways you can word it in 100 characters or less(if you can't get it down to 100 characters, get it as close as possible). Get as creative as you can. Ideally you want 8 different versions.

Also think about "advertising power words". These would be words like: new, save, safety, proven, love, discover, guarantee, health, results, you, secret, system, power, magic, immediate, insider, free, etc. Feel free to do a search for these power words and also "advertising power phrases", and use what you can in your ads without sounding like a greasy sales hack.

Another way to tackle this is to search for the top 100 advertising headlines, and choose a few that you can easily re-write in approximately 100 characters for your own business. This is a quick way, but it's a common "cheat" so your ads will be recognized as "copy-cats" by folks who are in the know. Use these only as a guide once you've done the USP homework. You'll know better how to rework them to your advantage if you've laid a great foundation.

You might think about different products in your company and write a USP for each one of them. Keep them short. We're going to turn these into ads for your Twitter stream, and they need to be short enough to share when you attach a URL to the end of them.

If one of your goals with Twitter is to gather leads make sure that most, if not all, of these ads lead to a free download or an enticing paid product that builds your list.

So, clear your head, and your desk, download the worksheet, and get to it! Once you have 8 great ads I'll be able to show you how to start putting these to work for you.

Day 11:

Auto-posting Your Ads to Twitter

Hopefully you have 8 great USP-based headlines that you can now turn into ads for Twitter.

You want to have all of these ads listed on a document. At the end of each ad put a bit.ly URL link to the appropriate page. This way the link isn't taking up too much space, and you can track how many people click on them.

Here's how you set this up:

➤ Go to www.Tweetspinner.com The box that comes up on that page is for their newsletter. You don't need any more spam in your inbox, so click the link that says "skip this step".

➤ Fill in the information to "create your account now".

➤ Confirm your account through your email and log in.

➤ Connect your Tweetspinner account to your Twitter account.

➤ Click "Timezone" in the top right hand corner and set your time zone.

➤ Click the middle tab that says "Smart Tweets".

➤ Click "Add Multiple Tweets".

➤ Paste the list of 8 ads in the box that appears and save the Tweetscheck to make sure none are too long).

➤ Look below the box and set it to post every 5 hours and NOT delete the list after it's done posting.

➤ Mark on your calendar to log in every 2 days and re-start the list by clicking "Save Schedule" On that same day you might want to check into bit.ly and see what ads are being clicked on regularly. This might help you adjust the less attractive ones to get more hits.

And we're done! A fairly easy task today after all the difficult ones behind you. Nice!

Day 12:

Setting Up Google Reader

We have one more task regarding the finding of great items to post on your Twitter page and then we'll start getting you some brilliant followers (no point in looking for followers if, when they check out your page, there's nothing interesting there!)

- Go to Google Reader (www.google.com/reader) and create an account, or log in with your Google information if you already have a Google account.

- In the left hand menu click "Browse for Stuff".

- Using your keywords, search to find great blogs and news sites that cater to your target market and your industry. You can also search for key people.

- Find a selection of 15-20 different sites at a minimum that have regular, helpful articles dealing with your target market and your industry. Avoid the ones you already have posting to your Twitter account. For each of these sites, click "subscribe".

- Once you've subscribed to as many great sites as you can find, close this down. It will work over the next week or so to gather a large selection of great articles for you which you will also program into your Twitter account. People will think you're amazing!

Day 13:

Setting Up Follow Automation

Your Twitter page is attractive, your bio is intriguing, your stream is now full of interesting, engaging Tweets. Today is the day we start setting up the systems to help you build and maintain that list of followers who will learn to love and adore you!

Today's task sets up the "rules" about who and how you follow so that it's all done automatically.

- ➤ Go to www.SocialOomph.com

- ➤ Click "Register" in the top right corner

- ➤ Fill in all your information and click "Create Free Account" at the bottom.

- ➤ Confirm your registration via email, and then log in.

- ➤ Once you're in go to the left menu bar and click "Social Accounts" Click "Add New Account" and click "Twitter" and follow the instructions for connecting your Twitter to your SocialOomph account.

- ➤ Go back to that same menu bar, click "Social Accounts" and then click "Edit Automation", and then next to your Twitter account click "Edit".

- ➤ Check the box that says "Automatically send a welcome message to new followers."

➢ Click the link below that says "How to rotate welcome messages (and why you should)." and follow the instructions for creating rotating welcome messages.

➢ Enter your messages in the box where it says "Send This Message"

➢ Check the box to auto-follow.

➢ Uncheck the box to vet your followers.

➢ Check to have an email sent when you get new followers.

➢ Click "save".

And you're done for the day! Congratulations!

Day 14:

Finding Followers Through Twitter Search

Woohoo! Time to get some followers to check out your AWESOME Twitter feed! Are you ready?

➢ Log in to your Twitter Account.

➢ In the search bar at the top of your Twitter page type in words that describe your ideal client. GET SPECIFIC! So, for example, if my target market is "stay at home moms in Seattle" I'd first do a search for "Stay at home mom" and then quickly go through the profiles to find any in Seattle. When I find one, I click on "follow". For Stay at home mom you also want to search SAHM. Then I might try "toddler" or "children" or "married". You can also search your keywords with hashtags, "#SAHM" for example, and that will show you the people who are talking about that topic.

➢ Search for your past and present clients, and for any future ones you may have your eye on, as well. And if you have friends or family who won't post embarrassing things about you, follow them, too,

➢ Keep working until you're following 50 people.

➢ Oh, and of course, do follow me @hotspotpromo. I'll follow you back!

And you're done! Congratulations! See you back here tomorrow!

Day 15:

Connecting With New Followers

After yesterday's efforts, I'm assuming you have a few new followers. Today you're going to let them know how delighted you are that they've shown up on your list.

- Go to your inbox and search for emails from Twitter. If your inbox is like mine, with hundreds of new emails every day, these can be easily overlooked. By searching for "Twitter" as "sender", they'll all show up in a nice, neat list.

- Start with the first one. Check out their Twitter page, and click on their link. If they offer a newsletter or a free download, get it, if you think it will help you build a relationship with them or help you move your business forward.

- Scan their Twitter and website for things you have in common.

- Send them a Tweet stating what you found out: "*Hey, @NewFollower, I also adore ice cream! My favourite is Maple Walnut - yours?*" for example. Make a connection using the things you have in common. Remember you've already thanked them for following automatically through SocialOoomph. This needs to be something different and personal.

- Here's an important note, though, always put the "@Twitterhandle" in the middle or end of your post. If you start the post with "@Twitterhandle" it is only seen by the person you're talking to and anyone you both follow. Get your engagement seen by everyone so you start to show up as a cool person to follow. Move your "@Twitter handle" to later in the post, or simply put a "." before the @ like this: ".@Twitterhandle"

➢ Continue doing this with each of your new followers.

This now becomes a daily activity. Schedule it somewhere in your day and keep it like you would any appointment. You're not likely to get hundreds of followers a day, so this is going to take, at most, about 30 minutes.

That's all for today. You should now do this every day before you start your assignment here, as part of your homework.

Day 16:

Finding Followers Through Twellow

Before you get started on today's assignment make sure you've connected with your new followers because I'm now going to help you get even more followers:

➢ Go to www.Twellow.com.

➢ Add yourself to the directory and fill out your profile. That way, people can find you.

➢ Now, using your keywords again, look for people in your target market. Also search for people in complimentary areas of business that you might be able to do joint ventures with.

➢ Follow those who fit the profile. Stop at around 50 people.

Let me just say a word here about the number of followers you have. For some people it's all about the numbers, and they boast about having 100,000 followers on Twitter or Facebook, or wherever. The truth is very few people can manage that number of followers well. You can do a much better job with fewer, targeted followers that you build a relationship with, than you can with thousands of followers who don't care two cents about you. Look for quality. Engage - I'll be showing you how to do that!

Day 17:

Daily Engagement Activities

Remember: before you get started on today's assignment, make sure you've connected with your new followers.

It's time now to just slow down a little with the whole building process, and learn to create ongoing connection with your Twitter family.

- Log in to Twitter.
- Set a timer for 5 minutes (I'm serious! You can get lost here!)
- Do a quick scan of your followers' Tweets:
    1. If you find anything worth re-tweeting fire one off by hovering your mouse over the Tweet, looking for the word "retweet", and clicking it.
    2. If someone shared one of your Tweets, say thank you.
    3. If you find anything you can comment on, comment.
    4. If someone has a problem, see if you can solve it - especially if you can use a resource from somewhere other than yourself to do it - then it won't look like you're shoving your business down their throat. Of course, if you can give them helpful advice for free, that makes you look good, too!
    5. If anyone deserves congratulations, congratulate them (great achievement, birthdays, anniversaries, etc).
    6. If anyone posts anything interesting that your followers would love, add it to your "TimelyTweets" list.

7. Chat about what you're currently up to - both business and some select personal things.

➢ When the timer beeps, stop.

➢ Schedule time in your day to do this two more times, 5 minutes only.

This also becomes a regular part of your routine. 45 minutes a day, maximum, on Twitter including three five-minute scans and 30 minutes to deal with new followers.

Once per week you have a longer run at it to handle the extras, like adding Tweets to Timely.is along with other tasks I'm about to show you. Set up an appointment for this in your day. I get up really early and get it done before the day starts.

And that's it! Great job!

Day 18:

Setting Up Tweetdeck

WAIT! Before you get started on today's assignment, make sure you've connected with your new followers and done a quick scan.

We're going to set up a new account today that will help you keep track of your Twitter in a much easier way.

- ➢ Go to www Tweetdeck.com and set up an account, and connect it to your Twitter account.

- ➢ Run the program.

- ➢ The "Settings" window will open - click on the "Accounts" button on the left.

- ➢ Add in your Facebook and LinkedIn accounts if you have them.

- ➢ Also look for "services" and put your bit.ly information in there:

    1. Log in to your bit.ly account.

    2. Click the drop-down arrow at the top right of your page next to your avatar.

    3. Click "Settings" and scroll down to "API Key" and copy that number.

    4. Go back to Tweetdeck and paste it in.

- At the top of the application you'll see a "+" sign in a circle. Click that.

- Click "Core".

- Click the columns you want to show (I suggest "All friends", "Mentions", and "Direct Messages" to start with. Choose any others that have meaning for you).

- Under "Groups/Lists" you can create other lists where you can group people such as "Prospects", "Competition", "Influencers" or according to complementary industries, or however else you might want to organize your Twitter followers. Each time you set up a list you can select which followers you want to have in that list.

- You can also set up certain searches so you can have "#help" or "#Golfnut" or any other searches you did to find people in the first place, so you can keep ongoing searches happening. As people show up here, you can follow them.

Set these up now and we'll use them more tomorrow. However, be careful not to get too crazy with the lists. 5-8 is probably about all you can reasonably handle.

Once you've done all that, you're done for the day!

Day 19:

Creating Twitter Lists

Remember to start by connecting with new followers, and doing a quick scan.

Yesterday we set up a bunch of lists. Today we're going to sort our new people into those lists.

- ➢ Open Tweetdeck.

- ➢ Go to your Direct Messages column.

- ➢ Start with the first post, and click on the name the message was sent to. This will open the person's information in a column.

- ➢ Go to the bottom of the column and click the little box with the people in it.

- ➢ A box will open up where you'll see your list of lists. Choose the list this person should belong to.

- ➢ Go back to direct messages, delete that post, and continue with the next person.

Work on this for 10 minutes, at three different times today. This should get you pretty close to having all your friends in lists and easy to manage.

Include this task as part of your connecting with new people. This will make using your Twitter that much easier.

Day 20:

Scheduling Google Reader Articles With Hootsuite

Before you get started on today's assignment, make sure you've connected with your new people and sorted them into lists. Also do a quick scan of your lists and engage with your followers (remember, set your alarm for 5 minutes for this part so you don't get sucked in).

We're going to add the final layer of automation today by connecting those great articles that your Google reader is finding to your Twitter stream. It's a little fiddly to start with, but after you do it a couple of times you'll sail through. Take a deep breath, relax your shoulders, and jump in!

- Go to Google Reader (www.google.com/reader) and log in.

- On the left-hand menu at the top click "all items" (if this looks funny when you open it you might need to change browsers).

- Scan through the article headings, looking for anything that might be interesting to your followers. When you find something you'd like to share, click the arrow at the far right of the article title you like and open it in a new tab.

- Once you've opened all the articles you're interested in click "Mark All As Read" in your Google reader (link is in the middle above the article list) and close down the reader.

- Open each tab and click on your bit.ly bookmarklet to open up the window with the post title and bit.ly link. Open this in all tabs first as it will save you time.

- Now, in a new tab, go to www.Hootsuite.com and open an account, confirm your email, and log in.

- Connect Hootsuite to any Social Media accounts that you have. You can connect up to 5 with the free account.

- On the left-hand menu near the top you'll see "publisher" - click that and leave it open in your browser.

- Scan the article to make sure you *do* want to share it. If not, close down the tab and move to the next one. If so, copy the information from the bit.ly window and go back to Hootsuite.

- At the top of the "Publisher" page in Hootsuite you'll see a box at the top left of the page that has "compose message" in it. Paste your bit.ly message in there, reformatting it if necessary.

- Next to the message box you'll see a drop-down menu for the social sites you connected to Hootsuite. Select where you want this to post by clicking on the icons.

- Back in the box where you pasted your text you'll see a calendar; click that and choose the time when you want your post to be Tweeted. I suggest you post your Tweets at approximately 9am, 1pm, 5pm, and 9pm. Don't get rigid here, just keep those times in mind as ballpark times.

- Click "schedule" under the box.

- Keep going until you've used up all the great articles you found, posting 4 per day. Ideally you have enough feeds to bring you at least 1 week's worth of posts (24-28 posts per week).

- When you've scheduled them all, close this down, and mark in your calendar a regular time to attend to this every week or two weeks, depending on how many feeds you have and how many great articles they provide.

Personally I have mine set up weekly and usually try to complete about 8-10 days at a time. That way I have some leeway should life get busy. Once you have the rhythm of this, you should be able to complete it in about 30 minutes per week.

Whew! That's done! I think you've earned a coffee!

Day 21:

Catch Up and Connect

I think it would be a good idea to use today to catch up in case you didn't get completely finished with yesterday's task, and also to spend time getting to know your followers.

So, today let's just:

- ➤ Connect with all your new folk and make them feel welcome and valued.
- ➤ Make sure you've got everyone sorted into lists.
- ➤ Find great things to comment on, re-tweet, and acknowledge.
- ➤ Finish up anything that still hasn't been completed.

Ahhh. Relaaaaax. Enjoy what you've accomplished so far!

We'll see you back here tomorrow!

Day 22:

Cleaning Out Your Follower List

Hello again! Once you've connected with your new followers and done a quick scan, we'll get started working on keeping your Twitter follower list clean.

Twitter has a number of funny little rules. One is you can only Follow 10% more people than are following you in order to keep spammers somewhat under control.

However, it means that those who are building their lists can quickly get into trouble if people aren't following them back. Of course, this shouldn't happen if you're tweeting quality Tweets and being as engaging and gracious as I've been teaching you.

Because of this, while you're building your initial list it's a good idea to keep an eye on people who aren't following you. Simply unfollow those people unless they bring you quality posts that are beneficial to you in some way.

Also, you'll find pretty quickly that there are spammers out there who follow you just to post ads. You want to get rid of those, too! Here's how:

- ➢ For the first group use a tool like www.Manageflitter.com to find out who isn't following you, and unfollow them.

- ➢ For the second group, simply "block and report spam" (check their stream by clicking on their name to make sure they really are continuously spamming). You do this in Tweetdeck by hovering your mouse over their picture, and clicking the little cog wheel, selecting "user" and then "block and report spam".

- If the user is simply uninteresting to you, click their name and "unfollow" at the bottom of the column that opens up.

Make sure you read and understand conditions and rules for following and unfollowing before you get going on this so you don't cross any lines. Also, once you hit 500 followers you can stop this gathering new followers and unfollowing non-followers, and let your list grow more organically. Just keep tossing the spammers out and those who simply don't add anything to your value like those who are always tweeting about non-essentials, or are rude or whatever else you don't like having in your stream.

So, having said that, today's task is to:

- Read and understand conditions and rules for following and unfollowing (support.twitter.com/articles/68916-following-rules-and-best-practices)

- Go to www.Manageflitter.com, connect your Twitter, and work through unfollowing those non-essential accounts that are not following you back, so you have more room to follow new people.

- Go to Tweetdeck and block any spammers. These are usually easy to find because they tend to have the "egg head" instead of a picture. Be careful, though, I follow some great accounts that unfortunately don't have photos.

- Toss those that are uninteresting to you

- Schedule this task to happen every second week, alternating with finding new followers.

- Stop all of this when you hit 500 followers. If you're doing a great job of the connecting your account should continue to grow on its own. When it's growing organically, you don't need to worry about unfollowing, but I'd continue to keep an eye on spam and toss it out.

And another day is done! See you back here tomorrow

Day 23:

Tweet Your Old Posts

Another gentle nudge: remember that before you get started on today's assignment you need to make sure you've connected with your new followers and put them into their lists. Today's task is short and sweet to give you lots of time to do this well.

If you have a Wordpress blog you want to go to your plug-ins and do a search for "Tweet Old Post" and install it to your blog.

Once it's installed on your blog go to the left-hand menu in your Wordpress back office, and below the settings tab you'll see a tab for setting this up. Click it, and decide which categories you want or don't want retweeted, how old the posts should be, and how often they should be re-tweeted. Now you'll see these posts coming up again on your Twitter stream to keep those old posts alive and well.

Just make sure you're re-tweeting posts that don't get old or have outdated information.

Ah - a nice easy day for you! Spend the extra time connecting on Twitter.

Day 24:

Create a Twitter Poll

Before you get started on today's assignment, make sure you've connected with your new followers and have them sorted into lists. Also do a quick scan and engage (remember to set your timer!)

Let's get some fun happening on your Twitter stream. Why not set up a poll for your followers to participate in? Think about starting with fun questions that have to do with your industry, but not really serious marketing. Do a search for "fun poll questions" or even search for "using polls to build your business" to get yourself started. Keep the questions simple.

Once you have some good ideas for questions, go to www.twitip.com and follow the very clear instructions for setting up a poll.

Try putting these together about once a month. Maybe offer a prize, but make sure you are following Twitter contest guidelines (support.twitter.com/articles/68877-guidelines-for-contests-on-twitter) if you do.

Make sure it's fun! If you get a great reputation for interesting, fun polls you'll be able to switch up from time to time with good questions that will help your business.

Have fun with this!

Tomorrow we'll learn about some other interesting things we can do with our followers.

Day 25:

Share a Picture

Have you connected with your new followers and filed them into lists? Have you done your 5 minute scan and engage? Then you're ready to move on!

Let's get creative today, and take a few pictures that you can share on Twitter. Nothing too personal, but perhaps you had a fantastic meal and you want to give a shout out to the restaurant and make sure you attach their Twitter handle! Or maybe it's a beautiful day and you take a picture and share that. Perhaps you saw the first Robin of Spring, or you found a funny sign, or something else significant.

To get started, take a walk today and look for things you can snap and share. When you get back home:

- Upload your photo onto your computer.
- Go to Tweetdeck.
- Click the square box with a pencil (yellow, top left) and open the status window.
- Type in a description or caption for your picture.
- Click the camera on the far right of the status box and find your photo and attach it.

You can also program pictures to post in Hootsuite by clicking the paper clip under the status window and attaching the file. These can be fun to share if you don't overdo it. Perhaps once or twice a week.

If you're a photographer/artist you might do it more often - like a "picture of the day" and post it at different times on different days to catch different people.

So, out you go with your camera, and find something worth sharing!

Day 26:

Join Klout

Before you get started on today's assignment, make sure you've connected with your new followers and you have them assigned to lists. Also do your quick 5-minute scan and engage.

Our assignment today is going to help us get greater visibility and "clout". Here's how you do it:

➢ Go to www.Klout.com and click "Understanding Klout" in the top right corner. Go through those pages so you know what this is about. The menu is on the left hand side.

➢ When you've clicked through all the pages, click the Klout logo at the top left and connect with your Twitter account.

➢ Retweet your Klout score if you like.

➢ Click "home" and see if you can give someone else a boost under the "Has Your Network Influenced You Recently?" heading.

➢ Now look at Klout's suggestions below that and connect with those with Klout in your area of focus.

There are different camps on the value of Klout. Some say it's useless, others say it's a great tool. I like to use it as a general guide to keep track of where I am. This isn't a hugely important site, but it helps people find you if they're looking for someone with your influence. It also helps you see if what you think is your area of influence, actually is. The other day Klout sent me an update saying I was now considered influential on the topic of broccoli. Hmmm. Don't take it too seriously. Just keep half an eyeball peeled to get a sense of where you're at. Schedule time into your calendar for this every month or so.

Regularly work to raise your Klout score by doing what I suggest in this book, and by rigorously unfollowing those that add no value to your Twitter stream. The more your Twitter stream reflects your business interests (though you do need to keep some of the personal stuff happening) the higher your Klout score.

Spend the rest of your time connecting and engaging.

Another nice short one, today! You should be starting to feel quite confident with your Twitter account now, and beginning to see some great results.

Day 27:

Adjusting Tweets Through Timely.is

Have you connected with your new followers and gotten them sorted into lists? Have you done your quick, 5-minute scan and engage? If so, you're ready to jump into today's lesson.

We're going to log back into Timely.is today and take a look at things.

- ➢ Log in and check to make sure you have enough posts in the system, in case you haven't checked in a while.

- ➢ Click "Performance" and take a look at the kinds of Tweets that are being clicked on and shared. See if there's a way you can adjust your next batch of Tweets to include more like these, in order to get you more exposure and engagement.

Again, a fairly easy lesson today to give you more time to work with your followers.

Day 28:

Create an Online Newspaper

I'm assuming by now I don't have to remind you to check in with your newest followers and get them on a list, or remind you to do your quick, 5-minute scan and engage, right?

So here's a fun assignment for today. Create a Paper.li newspaper of the most important posts in your area of interest.

- ➤ Go to www.Paper.li and connect with your Twitter account.

- ➤ Click on "Start Your Paper".

- ➤ Click on the big blue button to create a diverse newspaper.

- ➤ You'll see a list with 7 different content streams to choose from. Start by naming your newspaper using your main keyword as part of the title (fitness, golf, small business...) Think about the work you did on your USP and come up with something intriguing for your title.

- ➤ Now go to The Listorious 140 Lists (www.listorious.com/top/lists)and choose a list or two to follow that will make your paper of benefit to those you are trying to draw into your circle. When you find the list

    1. Click on the name, right click on "follow" and then select "copy link address".

    2. Click "Add" on paper.li.

    3. Paste in the URL in the format requested.

4. It's a good idea to connect with those who are listed in these lists, as well.

➢ Get a list of your best keywords and add them into "Keywords on Twitter".

➢ Copy those same keywords into "keywords on Facebook" and "Keywords on Google+" and include any RSS feeds you want. You can use the ones you have in Twitterfeed as a starting place.

➢ Of course, make sure your own posts and articles are in there through your Twitter feed or your blog feed. Also include your promo videos or whatever else you can find - just don't make the paper all about you. Get your readers used to seeing you in the middle of all these great names!

➢ Scroll down and check the appropriate boxes, fill out anything pertinent and click "Save".

➢ Once it's published you can delete/re-arrange the stories to suit your needs/desires. Tweak this to make sure your BEST stories are at the top. This makes your paper something invaluable to your followers.

➢ Entice your readers to check out your paper by publishing it with a great headline to draw them in.

➢ You can also use this to dominate your niche market. If one of your followers raises an issue or asks a question that your paper answers, send them a Tweet that says something like "Hi, @TwitterHandle! @SavvyUser has a great article on (name topic/issue) here: (Link to Your Paper.li)"

➢ Finally, use this paper to stay on top of trends in your industry.

Now it will do a search for that daily, and when something great shows up in your search it will automatically publish it as an online newspaper and you simply post it to your Twitter. You can continue to play with this by clicking "settings" in the drop-down box next to your avatar in the top right corner.

And that's today's task finished. Have fun with this!

Day 29:

Set Up a Listening a Listening Station

Before you get started on today's assignment, make sure you've connected with your new followers and done your scan and engage.

We're going to expand the use of your Google Reader to set up a listening station for your business. This will enable you to see whenever someone is talking about you, your business, your industry, and any of your keywords. Knowing what's going on will enable you to respond immediately to compliments or problems that arise. You'll also be able to keep tabs on changes and important announcements in your industry.

You already have some of this in place, but now you want to create Google alerts to follow important words. Let's do that now:

- Go to www.google.com/alerts and log in.

- Add in the search term (see below) and leave everything else as it is, except that you need to change "How Many" to "All". You can change this later if it's too much or a lot of useless results, but start here. Set "deliver to" to "feed" so it goes to your Google reader.

- Here are some ideas for alerts that you need to set up:

    1. Follow your keywords.

    2. Follow your name.

    3. Follow your company name.

4. Follow brand-related mentions.

5. Follow your website addresses (URLs).

6. Follow your competitors' names.

7. Follow the conversations and names of the people or representatives on your team that are active online.

8. Follow industry and opportunity phrases: if you're selling insurance, you might look for phrases like "need insurance coverage" or "shopping for car insurance". If you're in weight loss, look for "I need to lose a few pounds", etc.

➤ Now, once this is set up, you need to use it!

1. Find out what folks are already doing in your industry. Where are the holes? What are the questions that need to be answered? What are the issues that come up over and over and over? Start thinking through these things and begin to design a strategy for meeting the needs that are coming up in your listening station.

2. Find out what your competition is doing - can you capitalize on that? Improve on it? Learn from it?

3. Use it for customer service in case someone's complaining about you, your business or your industry. Jump in and solve the issue or point them to a solution.

4. Use it to connect to people who are influential in your industry that you haven't connected with yet.

And you're done. We'll see you back here tomorrow for the next lesson!

Day 30:

Becoming Influential

By now you should be fairly adept at using Twitter for your business.

Now you need to understand how to move forward in order to both become a person of influence, and to create influencers in your followers who will "evangelize" for you. To accomplish this you need to focus on reaching up and reaching out.

Reaching Up:

As you go about your daily Twitter duties watch those people who carry influence in your industry and target market. Start becoming an "evangelist" for their business: re-tweet their posts, comment on their Tweets with something useful or worthy, answer a question, share a passion. Don't just "suck up", become a useful part of their Twitter inner circle, and you'll notice that they'll start engaging with you more often. When that happens, others will see it, and you will become someone to watch. Again, don't just do this superficially. Do this with passion and make sure you're always adding value. Don't do this with everyone. Choose about 3-5 top influencers in your industry or area of expertise, and work hard at those. Here are some ideas for doing that:

> ➢ Start by creating a Twitter list of people you are considering as the influential heavy-hitters in your target market and industry.

- Watch them for a while in this list to see how they interact, with whom they interact, and why they interact. This will help you understand how best to get their attention when the time comes to reach out.

- Find and follow those users who are already engaging with your target market and in your industry. Observe and learn from them as well.

- As you find the best people move them to a new list so you can better keep track of what they're doing and find the best opportunities to "jump in".

- Create a Paper.li with just these people, add something valuable from yourself, give it a hot title, and then share this around to others. Mention the contributors in your paper with an @ mention to bring it to their attention: "*Wow, great posts today in "Social Media Superstars"! Check out what @TwitterHandle1, @TwitterHandle2 and @TwitterHandle3 have to say!*" Worded like this all of your followers and all of their followers will see it.

- Use www.Favstar.fm to find your influencer's most popular Tweets and simply retweet them. You do this by going to favstar and in the top search bar put in their Twitter username. When their page comes up, under the title you'll see "Most Favorited Tweets" and "Most Retweeted Tweets". Choose a couple every few days from each of your influencers to retweet.

- Study their favourite Tweets, and create your own to match. Don't copy, find out what they like and create that kind of Tweet. You find their favourite Tweets by going to http://twitter.com/#!/TwitterHandle/favorites (for example: http://twitter.com/#!/hotspotpromo/favorites). Feel free to retweet their favourites as well, but mostly use this to find out how best to engage their attention.

- Tweet about them, preferably something accurate, favourable and helpful, and share their wisdom with your world.

- Leave useful comments on their blogs.

- Find communities they are a part of and join in if possible. but don't become a stalker or a nuisance!

- Don't just stick to Twitter to find the top influencers in your industry. Check out a tool like www2.mblast.com, www.ecairn.com, www.grouphigh.com to help you find relevant influencers, rate them, group them, contact them and follow up. Also, search www.alltop.com, www.BlogCatalog.com, and www.Alexa.com to determine who has an influential blog in your field.

Reaching Out

Reaching out is what you're already doing on Twitter with all the engagement ideas I've been teaching you (which reminds me, don't forget to connect with your new followers and do your quick scan and engage!) The best part is that when the reaching up starts to get noticed by the right people, your followers will notice, too, and their estimation of you will rise. If all you're doing is sucking up to the big guy you will find their interest waning quite quickly.

With all that being said, today you simply need to set up your Twitter so you are ready to observe and watch. You'll know best when the time is right to jump in and engage these heavy hitters!

Tomorrow we wrap all this up with some fun stuff!

Day 31:

What Else Can I Do With Twitter?

Here we are at the last lesson! I hope you've found this helpful and enlightening, and I hope you've found it fairly easy to follow.

Let's look at what else you can do with Twitter. Depending on what you want to accomplish you can also:

- Tweet specials and promotions. Program these into TweetSpinner in place of/in addition to what you already have there, or you can just tweet them one-by-one.

- Lead people to specific web pages/landing pages to build your list.

- Post news and changes in your business.

- Check the "Trending Topics" on the RH side of your actual Twitter page and join the conversation.

- Solve problems and answer questions.

- Express an opinion on something. Don't worry about being controversial, just don't be rude or pig-headed.

- Share discoveries you've made about great tools, a wonderful book you've read. I'd be grateful if you'd share a link to this one!

- Ask your Twitter community for help in finding something or solving an issue.

- If you use "Remember the Milk" for your to-do list you can have it send reminders to Twitter through this link: www.RememberTheMilk.com/services/twitter

- You can update your Google Calendar with www.TwitterCal.com, a free service that allows you to add events to your Google Calendar from your Twitter client.

- Use a client called www.TwitterNotes.com to Tweet notes to yourself.

- Set an alarm and be informed via a Twitter Timer through www.retweet.com/timer

- Share your business card with www.twtBizCard. When you sign up, the service will pull in the data from your Twitter profile as starter information, and you can add other details to customize your card. Here's mine: www.twtbizcard.com/hotspotpromo. I personally don't use it much so I didn't pay the extra to have my logo on it. This is just the "bare bones" version.

- Use www.TweetPsych.com to analyze the personality traits of any public Twitter profile. Why not see what it says about you? Or even me? (hotspotpromo.com)

Most of all, have fun with this! You've worked hard to create a great presence here. Make sure you take time to enjoy it, too!

It's a Wrap!

Whew! We're done! Thanks for hanging in there with me through all of this. I hope you found it helpful, and not too overwhelming. If you have ideas for inclusion or improvement for a revised edition, feel free to pass them on via info@hotspotpromotion.com.

I'd be grateful if you'd help me spread the word about this book by sharing it on your Twitter and I'd be honoured to have your review which you can leave on the Amazon page. Your positive review can make a huge difference to the sales, which means I'll have enough money to create more guides like this! :)

If you want more marketing ideas, and to be kept in the loop for the rest of the books in this series, please sign up for our newsletter: "The Marketing Minute". You'll find the details on our homepage: www.HotSpotPromotion.com

Don't hesitate to contact us if you need any help at all with this or any other marketing challenge for your business. We are here to serve you! No need is too great, and no budget too small. Find out more about the kinds of things we can do to help on the next page.

Darlene Hull

HotSpotPromotion.com

How Might We Help You?

HotSpot Promotion is a marketing company that believes everyone deserves quality marketing! No need is too great, and no budget is too small.

HotSpot Promotion works hard for the "little guy" and we do everything possible to work within your limited budget and overcrowded calendar. Of course, we're also happy to handle larger companies as well. We are able to service anyone who needs a big or little boost in their visibility and business growth!

Whatever your goals, we'd love to come alongside and help you achieve them! HotSpot Promotion provides coaching, step-by-step instruction and practical, real-world guidance to help you get your business off the ground and we can help you in three different ways:

1. we can walk you through it yourself, showing you exactly what to do and how to do it.

2. we can let you do some and take the more complicated/time-consuming things off your hands, or

3. we can set it up, and manage it so that it's pretty much "hands off". You need to know, however, there are always some things you need to do yourself, but we'll show you how to do it in the least-complicated, most time/effort efficient way).

Here are some of the ways we can help you:

Get A FREE Success Strategy Blueprint

- ➢ Fill in our 80+ point questionnaire and we'll take a look and see what's going on in your business.

- We'll make note of what's working, what needs improvement, and share our results with you.

- We'll give you a suggested list of things to do in order of importance, complete with links and resources to help you do that on your own.

- Get the information on the sidebar of our website at www.HotSpotPromotion.com.

Website Design

All our websites are based on WordPress templates so your site is:

- affordable

- easy for you to manage yourself if you wish to

- easy to find someone to manage your site for you if you wish to go with someone other than HotSpot Promotion once it's set up

- easily expanded to grow with your business

- easily transported to different hosting plans if necessary

- entirely yours when it's done. You aren't locked into anything or forced to work within parameters that make you uncomfortable or that limit your business growth and expansion

Phenomenal Follow Up

If you have a drawer full of business cards, or contact information that you know you should do SOMETHING with, but you're just not sure WHAT, this service is for you.

Here are some amazing statistics from The National Sales Executive Association:

- 48% of sales people never follow up with a prospect
- 25% of sales people make a second contact and stop
- 12% of sales people make more than three contacts
- 2% of sales are made on the 1st contact
- 3% of sales are made on the 2nd contact
- 5% of sales are made on the 3rd contact
- 10% of sales are made on the 4th contact
- *80% of sales are made on the 5th-12th contact* (emphasis mine)

This is why you need follow up! We will work with you to set up a system that's 80% automated, very affordable, multi-touch, multi-tool, and fully personalized. It will turn your clients and prospects into raving fans and enthusiastic evangelists for your business. It will make you look pretty good, too!

Social Media Set-up and Maintenance

- We'll see what it is you do, and help you choose the best social media platforms to get your message out.
- We'll help you design a business strategy to get the best bang for your social media efforts.
- We'll get you set up in such a way that looking after your social media is simple, and easy to maintain.
- We'll take on as much or as little as you need to keep everything ticking along nicely.

- We'll create a unified, branded graphic presentation across all your social media sites so your clients instantly recognize you and know what it is you do.

Local and Mobile Marketing

- We'll claim your Google/Yahoo/Bing local business listing and optimize it for the best possible ranking.
- We'll help you create coupons to offer your clients.
- We'll gather and post reviews.
- We'll gather and post citations.
- We'll create a mobile landing page for your business with "click to call" or a coupon.
- We'll help you set up and track mobile advertising.
- We'll help you set up and use location apps to bring clients into your business "on demand".
- We'll set up and track SMS service/campaigns.
- We'll provide ongoing reviews so you can see how you're doing.

Graphic Design

- No online presence yet, or just need to "freshen up" what you have? Need graphics to get that done?
- We'll design a professional logo and integrate it into your WordPress website and your social media backgrounds.
- We'll design business cards to match.

Coaching

➢ Need help figuring it all out?

➢ We'll come alongside and coach you in the best way to get started with your marketing efforts.

➢ We create different discount packages for "one-off's", short-term, and long term, coaching, depending on the amount of coaching you need.

➢ We also create simple DIY resources (like this book) that can help you get the job done in your own time, with a very small price-tag.

For these services and any other marketing needs, or for any questions you might have please don't hesitate to contact us:

➢ Phone: 403-374-0167

➢ email: info@hotspotpromotion.com

About the Author

Darlene Hull is the Founder and President of HotSpotPromotion.com, a full-service marketing company specializing in the small and home business which she runs with her two home schooled teenagers.

Darlene tried almost every legal job known to man until she realized that she was not created to work for someone else. Her passion for all things entrepreneurial, the necessity of learning the skill of marketing for her own success, and her experience in so many different areas of business make Darlene an ideal champion for the small business owner.

A teacher by nature, Darlene loves to make the complicated simple and accessible to the overwhelmed and uninitiated.

Currently Darlene resides in the shadow of the Canadian Rockies with her husband, her son and daughter, and a Bichon Shih-tzu named Nicki.

Made in the USA
Charleston, SC
08 September 2012